Preventing Mass Atrocities

*From a Responsibility to Protect (RtoP)
to a Right to Assist (RtoA)
Campaigns of Civil Resistance*

Peter Ackerman and Hardy Merriman

ICNC
PRESS

Summary

The Responsibility to Protect (RtoP) was developed as a doctrine to prevent mass atrocities (genocide, ethnic cleansing, war crimes and crimes against humanity). Offering an important exception to the principle of nonintervention, it relies on the UN Security Council to authorize its most aggressive provisions such as armed intervention. Despite its initial promise, a decade of practice has revealed that RtoP can easily be curtailed by the objections of UN member states.

The world needs new approaches to atrocity prevention that are adaptable, innovative and independent of a state-centered doctrine. With the aim of reducing risk factors such as civil war, we argue for a new normative framework called The Right to Assist (RtoA), which would strengthen international coordination and support for nonviolent civil resistance campaigns demanding rights, freedom and justice against non-democratic rule. RtoA would:

1. engage a wide range of stakeholders such as NGOs, states, multilateral institutions and others;
2. bolster various factors of resilience against state fragility; and
3. incentivize opposition groups to sustain commitment to nonviolent strategies of change.

The adoption of this doctrine can reduce the probability of violent conflict that significantly heightens atrocity risk, while increasing the prospects for constructive human development.

Our argument is grounded in social science research about the impact of civil resistance on societies. We explain what makes civil resistance campaigns effective and offer a five-part typology of different forms of support for these campaigns. We then address questions about operationalizing the Right to Assist framework, including offering:

*   criteria to determine what civil resistance campaigns could be supported;
*   considerations in determining what forms of assistance to offer;
*   discussion of the intersection of external support and international law;
*   discussion of invocation, oversight, and implementation.

Our goal is to offer a specific framework for how, practically, RtoA could be implemented, and we invite additional research and debate to develop and refine ideas on this topic.

About the Authors

Dr. Peter Ackerman is the Founding Chair of the International Center on Nonviolent Conflict (ICNC) and co-author of the books *A Force More Powerful: A Century of Nonviolent Conflict* (2001) and *Strategic Nonviolent Conflict: The Dynamics of People Power in the Twentieth Century* (1994). He was Series Editor and Principal Content Advisor for the two-part Emmy-nominated PBS-TV series, "A Force More Powerful" which charts the history of civilian-based resistance in the 20th century. He was also Executive Producer of several other films on civil resistance, including the PBS-TV documentary, "Bringing Down a Dictator", on the fall of Serbian dictator Slobodan Milosevic, which received a 2003 Peabody Award and the 2002 ABC News VideoSource Award of the International Documentary Association. Dr. Ackerman serves as co-chair of the International Advisory Committee of the United States Institute for Peace and is on the Executive Committee of the Board of the Atlantic Council.

Hardy Merriman is President of the International Center on Nonviolent Conflict (ICNC). He has worked in the field of civil resistance since 2002, presenting at workshops for activists and organizers around the world; speaking widely about civil resistance movements with academics, journalists, and members of international organizations; and developing educational resources. His writings have been translated into numerous languages. From 2016-2018 he was also an adjunct lecturer at the Fletcher School of Law and Diplomacy (Tufts University). Mr. Merriman has contributed to the books *Is Authoritarianism Staging a Comeback?* (2015), *Civilian Jihad: Nonviolent Struggle, Democratization, and Governance in the Middle East* (2010), and *Waging Nonviolent Struggle: 20th Century Practice and 21st Century Potential* (2005) and co-authored two literature reviews on civil resistance. He has also written about the role of nonviolent action in countering terrorism and co-authored *A Guide to Effective Nonviolent Struggle*, a training curriculum for activists.

Table of Contents

Introduction 1

     RtoA as an Alternative Approach 3

How Support for Civil Resistance Campaigns Can Help Prevent Mass Atrocities 5

What Forms of Assistance are Helpful? 11

     1. Public Education about Civil Resistance 11

     2. Capacity Building for Civil Resistance Campaigns 13

     3. Mitigating the Impact of Repression and Disruption 14

     4. Raising the Cost of Repression 14

     5. Fostering a Stable Political Transition 16

     Applying this Framework: Re-examining Resistance and Possibilities in Syria 17

Addressing Concerns about a Right to Assist 20

     1. What campaigns should receive assistance? 20

     2. Is support for civil resistance synonymous with supporting regime change? 22

     3. What if external support has a harmful impact on a campaign? 23

     4. What if external support contributes to societal instability? 25

     5. What forms of external support to civil resistance campaigns are permissible under international law? 27

     6. How should RtoA be invoked, and who should exercise oversight? 30

Conclusion 34

Endnotes 37

Acknowledgments 59

Figures

Figure 1: Mass Killings in Violent and Nonviolent Campaigns 5

Figure 2: Historic Success Rates of Nonviolent and Violent Campaigns: 1900-2006 6

Figure 3: Probability that a Country will be a Democracy Five Years After a Campaign Ends: 1900-2006 7

Introduction

The end of the Cold War in 1991 led to optimism about the prospects for increased peace and security around the globe. Shortly thereafter the world witnessed atrocities in Bosnia (1993), Rwanda (1994) and Kosovo (1999). In each case the violence occurred with both domestic perpetrators and victims.

Consensus began building that an international response was needed that would require diluting the principle of nonintervention. A new doctrine called "The Responsibility to Protect" (RtoP) was adopted by the United Nations in 2005, stating that:

> Each individual state has the responsibility to protect its population from genocide, war crimes, ethnic cleansing and crimes against humanity. The international community should, as appropriate, encourage and help states to exercise this responsibility... and take collective action, in a timely and decisive manner through the Security Council, should peaceful means be inadequate....[1]

In 2009, RtoP was further developed to include three pillars for implementation, outlined as follows:

Pillar 1 – States have a responsibility to protect their citizens from mass atrocities

Pillar 2 – States commit to building the capacity of other states to prevent and protect their populations from mass atrocities

Pillar 3 – The UN Security Council may authorize external intervention if states fail to uphold their responsibility to protect their populations[2]

A major test of RtoP came when the UN Security Council passed Resolution 1973 on March 17, 2011. Based on the view that the Libyan government was imminently going to commit atrocities in the city of Benghazi, the UN Security Council approved a "no-fly zone" over Libya and authorized "all necessary measures to protect civilians."[3]

A few days later a foreign military campaign consisting exclusively of airpower began to carry out this Resolution. It repelled Libyan dictator Muammar Qaddafi's military and mercenaries but also enabled Libyan rebels to launch offensive operations on the ground and push toward the capital.[4] Qaddafi's government was subsequently toppled through violence and seven months later, he was captured and killed.

Scholars and members of the policy community disagree about the propriety of this intervention. Regardless of one's view, however, it is indisputable that the intervention resulted in significant loss of life. It did not stop violent conflict while Qaddafi remained in power, and it led to further violent conflict and regional instability after Qaddafi's ouster.[5] It also created damaging incentives for opposition groups in other countries (including those in Syria) to become violent in the hopes of prompting external armed intervention.[6]

In addition, leaders of aspiring nuclear states noted that Qaddafi—who had previously relinquished his nuclear weapons program in the face of western pressure—was ousted by NATO's Libya intervention and this impacted their calculations about whether to give up their own nuclear ambitions in the future.[7]

Because of the precedent it set, the Libya intervention also severely damaged the prospects for Pillar 3 of RtoP to be invoked in the future. When NATO expanded the mandate of Resolution 1973 from a no-fly zone to regime change, the Chinese and Russian governments made it clear that they would never allow the Security Council to authorize anything similar to this again.[8] In subsequent years, severe mass atrocities in Syria, Central African Republic, South Sudan and Myanmar unfolded with no prospect for armed intervention under RtoP.

As RtoP's third pillar has become untenable, more recent thinking has focused on the use of Pillar 2, which aims to build the capacity of states to prevent and protect their populations from atrocities. However, Pillar 2 is limited by the fact that it can be operationalized only through the consent of a host government. As such, any government can disallow support to protect its population if it feels that the support may challenge its own practices and policies. Furthermore, some governments may deliberately refuse support under Pillar 2 because they want to commit or enable mass atrocities, with little fear that Pillar 3 could now be invoked against them.

Thus from its original adoption to the present, RtoP has been damaged and its fundamental weaknesses revealed. It is constrained within a state-centered framework, depending on the UN Security Council to authorize its most aggressive provisions, and the consent of host governments to allow other forms of support.

The risk of mass atrocities is too stark for debate to remain stuck in this conundrum. We need new approaches to prevention that are more adaptive, innovative and independent of a state-centered doctrine. In this paper we argue for one such approach: international support for populations that are waging nonviolent civil resistance to win rights, freedom

> *From its original adoption to the present, the Responsibility to Protect has been damaged and its fundamental weaknesses revealed.*

and justice against non-democratic rule. To this end, we propose a new normative framework called The Right to Assist (RtoA), under which a variety of actors—NGOs, states, multilateral institutions and others—can organize such efforts without relying on the UN or foreign governments for official authorization or implementation. RtoA can incentivize opposition groups to sustain commitment to nonviolent strategies of change, thus reducing the probability of civil war and atrocities, and increasing the probability of democratic outcomes.

RtoA as an Alternative Approach

The Right to Assist is based on the premise that the risk of atrocities rises dramatically when two or more sides engage in violent conflict. For example, approximately two-thirds of mass atrocities between 1945-2010 took place in the context of civil wars.[9] Therefore, if we want to reduce the amount of atrocities in the world, we need to reduce the probability of violent conflict as a response to intrastate disputes.[10]

Non-democratic governments heighten the risk of violent conflict.[11] The repression, misrule, lack of accountability and lack of respect for rights that characterize these regimes lead to simmering resentment among the populations they rule. Frequently, popular grievances are driven or compounded by government incompetence, corruption and inequitable distribution of resources.

Left on their own, such governments rarely self-democratize. Far more often their populations find their rule intolerable and eventually start to rise up and resist. When populations do this (and it is more a question of *when*, not *if*), they face a pivotal choice of how they will resist: through violent or nonviolent tactics.

The last three decades reveal that people are increasingly choosing nonviolent tactics and waging campaigns of civil resistance (sometimes referred to as "nonviolent campaigns", "civil resistance movements" or "people power movements").[12] These campaigns are driven by large numbers of ordinary people employing a range of tactics—such as strikes, boycotts, civil disobedience, mass demonstrations, acts of noncooperation and various other nonviolent actions—to fight for rights, freedom and justice.

It may seem counterintuitive that such campaigns can succeed against authoritarian rule, but extensive practice reveals that they drive up a government's costs of control (politically, economically and socially) and expose cracks in the loyalties and interests of various groups in society. In the face of sustained, organized and widespread noncooperation and

> *Both violent and nonviolent resistance increase societal instability, but the risk of resulting atrocities is vastly higher for violent insurgency than it is for civil resistance.*

dissent, defections by those within a government's pillars of support become far more likely. Rulers may opt to make concessions and reforms as a way to shore up their position, but if they instead increasingly rely on violent repression, popular civil resistance can eventually make their oppressive system unsustainable. As a regime's societal and institutional base dissolves, commands are no longer followed and rulers are left with no other option than to step down.

How Support for Civil Resistance Campaigns Can Help Prevent Mass Atrocities

Both violent and nonviolent resistance increase societal instability, but the risk of resulting atrocities is vastly higher for violent insurgency than it is for civil resistance. We should therefore find ways to incentivize and support the choice of civil resistance.

A 2018 study by scholars Evan Perkoski and Erica Chenoweth highlights this risk differential. They find that in aggregate, 43 percent of national uprisings (using either violent or nonviolent tactics) are subject at some point to mass killings (in which 1,000 or more noncombatant civilians are intentionally killed in a single, continuous event). However, the type of resistance being waged has a major impact on this probability. Violent campaigns were subject to mass killings nearly three times as often as nonviolent campaigns were (68 percent vs. 23 percent).[13] This finding is critical, because unlike certain structural risk factors (such as the presence of an autocratic government, elite ethnicity, or exclusionary ideology) that are immovable in the short term, resistance type can be directly and immediately influenced by opposition groups on the ground, as well as by external actors.[14]

Figure 1: Mass Killings in Violent and Nonviolent Campaigns

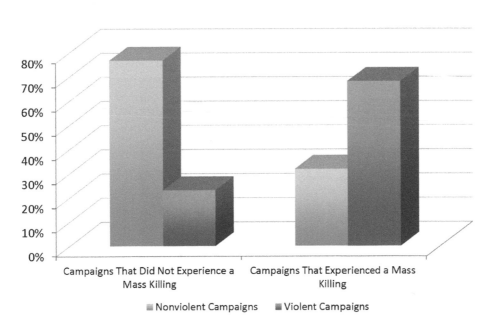

Source: Perkoski, Evan, and Erica Chenoweth. (2018) *Nonviolent Resistance and Prevention of Mass Killings During Popular Uprisings*. Washington, DC: ICNC Press.

Beyond directly reducing the risk of mass killings, civil resistance is also far more likely to lead to a democratic political transition than violent campaigns or top-down, elite-driven efforts.[15] As such, civil resistance has greater potential to reduce other factors that heighten atrocity risk (e.g. non-democratic rule and its frequent correlates: impunity and lack of civilian control of security forces, lack of rule of law, corruption, resource inequality and marginalization of certain groups in society), while bolstering factors (such as democracy, good governance, and a strong civil society) that lead to resilience.[16]

Here is what the data shows about the efficacy and impacts of violent and nonviolent campaigns:

1. Nonviolent civil resistance campaigns are more than twice as likely as violent insurgencies to achieve political transitions

An award-winning 2011 study by scholars Erica Chenoweth and Maria Stephan evaluated the effectiveness of 323 violent and nonviolent campaigns seeking maximalist objectives (a change of government, expulsion of foreign occupiers, or self-determination) between 1900-2006.[17] Defying the conventional wisdom, their data showed that nonviolent campaigns achieved political transitions 53 percent of the time versus 26 percent of the time for violent campaigns.[18]

Figure 2: Historic Success Rates of Nonviolent and Violent Campaigns: 1900-2006

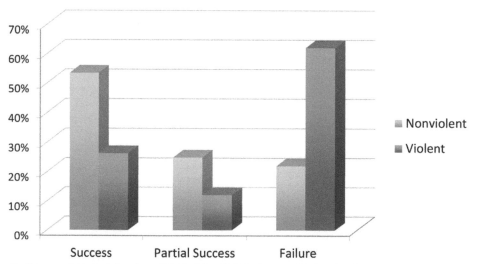

Source: Chenoweth, Erica, and Maria J. Stephan. (2011). *Why Civil Resistance Works: The Strategic Logic of Nonviolent Conflict.* New York: Columbia University Press.

2. Successful civil resistance campaigns are vastly more likely to yield durable democratic gains than violent insurgencies or top-down transitions driven by elites

Chenoweth and Stephan further examined the outcomes of nonviolent and violent campaigns five years after they ended. They found that political transitions driven by civil resistance led to democratic outcomes 57 percent of the time, versus 6 percent for transitions driven by armed insurgency.[19]

Remarkably, they also found that even failed civil resistance campaigns could plant the seeds for democratic development down the road. When civil resistance campaigns dissolved before achieving a political transition, there remained a 35 percent probability of an emergent democratic outcome in the ensuing five years.[20]

Figure 3: Probability that a Country will be a Democracy Five Years After a Campaign Ends: 1900-2006

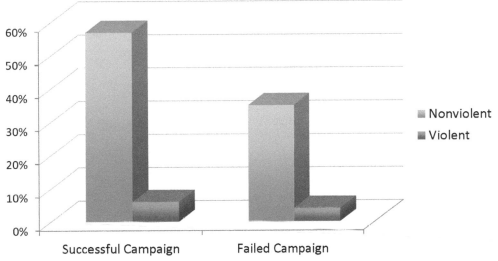

Source: Chenoweth, Erica, and Maria J. Stephan. (2011). *Why Civil Resistance Works: The Strategic Logic of Nonviolent Conflict.* New York: Columbia University Press.

Findings of a strong relationship between civil resistance, democratization and other factors of stability have been replicated over numerous other studies.[21] Most recently, scholar Jonathan Pinckney compared transitions driven by civil resistance against those driven by violent insurgency or top-down political changes (such as coups or elite-led liberalization). He found that 74 percent of transitions driven by civil resistance ended in democracies, versus 29 percent for transitions that were not driven by civil resistance.[22]

3. Civil resistance campaigns can succeed against even highly powerful and authoritarian adversaries

A frequent response to the discrepancy in success rates and outcomes of violent and nonviolent campaigns is an assertion that violent campaigns emerge in more challenging contexts and confront more challenging regimes. However, the data unequivocally rebuts this claim. Examining 323 violent and nonviolent campaigns, Chenoweth and Stephan evaluated the conditions under which campaigns emerge and succeed and concluded that:

> The evidence suggests that civil resistance is often successful regardless of environmental conditions that many people associate with the failure of nonviolent campaigns.[23]

> ... the vast majority of nonviolent campaigns have emerged in authoritarian regimes... where even peaceful opposition against the government may have fatal consequences.

> ... even when we control for the target regime type, nonviolent resistance remains significant in improving the odds of success.... Therefore, whether the opponent is democratic or nondemocratic seems to matter little with regard to the success of nonviolent campaigns.[24]

Pinckney finds that:

> ... civil resistance transitions do not take place in systematically more... [democratic] environments than other kinds of transitions....

> ... even in very unfavorable conditions, initiating a political transition through nonviolent resistance is much more likely to lead to democracy than initiating a transition through violence, top-down liberalization, or external intervention.[25]

Chenoweth and Stephan also examined the impact of state power on campaign emergence and outcomes, and concluded that:

> ... the power of the state in question does not determine whether a campaign that emerges is nonviolent or violent. Most notably, nonviolent campaigns emerge in some of the most objectively powerful states in the world....
>
> Interestingly, we also find no relationship between the... [the state's] capabilities and the probability of [campaign] success.... Nonviolent resistance continues to be effective regardless of how powerful the opponent state is...."

This research reveals civil resistance to be a potent force, capable of confronting and transforming even entrenched and violent rulers, at success rates far higher than alternative means of transition.

It is not the role of outsiders to try to create campaigns of civil resistance, but when ordinary people under non-democratic rule decide to rise up, the choice of civil resistance should be incentivized and supported. External assistance can further help people sustain their commitment to nonviolent tactics. This will minimize the risk of atrocities.

> *When ordinary people under non-democratic rule decide to rise up, the choice of civil resistance should be incentivized and supported.*

At the same time, providing external assistance to these campaigns requires further clarification of a number of issues. First, what forms of assistance are helpful? Second, how can some potential concerns and questions about RtoA be addressed, including:

1. What campaigns should receive assistance?

2. Is support for civil resistance synonymous with supporting regime change?

3. What if external support has a harmful impact on a campaign?

4. What if external support contributes to societal instability?

5. What forms of external support to civil resistance campaigns are permissible under international law?

6. How should RtoA be invoked, and who should exercise oversight?

The remainder of this paper will address these questions.

What Forms of Assistance are Helpful?

External support to civil resistance campaigns under RtoA must be premised on an understanding of what makes such campaigns effective.

We can examine this issue in two ways: first, by looking at the role of conditions in a campaign's environment (commonly referred to as "structural conditions"), and second, by looking at the skills and choices of participants within a campaign.

The conventional wisdom is that structural conditions determine a campaign's emergence and outcome. However, research points to a different conclusion—that the choices and skills of civil resisters can have a significant impact on a campaign's development and trajectory. Quantitative and qualitative research informs us that nonviolent campaigns have arisen and triumphed in the face of powerful, non-democratic regimes that are willing to use repression.[26] They have also emerged and succeeded in diverse societies and countries with various levels of economic development.[27] Although not every condition in a campaign's environment has been tested, we can infer from available findings that just as skills and strategy matter in other kinds of contests (electoral, business or military, for example), they also matter in civil resistance. The capacity of resisters to unify, plan, mobilize, prioritize goals, sequence tactics, develop effective communications, maintain nonviolent discipline, and make other strategic choices can be critical in overcoming adverse conditions and creating campaign outcomes.

Understanding civil resistance as a contest—in which either side in a conflict can prevail if it remains united, organized and strategic in its actions—can help to orient external support. More research on this topic is merited and currently in progress, but existing case history offers a list of several different categories of assistance that can make an impact.[28] These include:

1. Public Education about Civil Resistance
When a population rises up against an authoritarian regime, people in that population face the choice of whether to employ violent or nonviolent tactics. We know that when

people feel fundamentally threatened, they tend to engage in the form of resistance that seems most powerful to them. Too frequently violent insurrection is perceived as their only viable option. Criticisms of choosing violence and calls for peace will not change this unless a viable alternative means of struggle is offered.[29]

Public education efforts can spread awareness that civil resistance is an option with a much higher success rate and better long-term outcomes than violence. In addition, civil resistance has far broader appeal—nonviolent movements can enlist the support and participation of a wider demographic (men, women, parents, elders, children and others) than violence, which is often marketed narrowly to men and sometimes women of fighting age. Accordingly, Chenoweth finds that "The average nonviolent campaign is about 11 times as large (as a proportion of the population) than the average violent campaign."[30] There are also much lower barriers to enter a civil resistance campaign than a violent insurgency. For example, people may participate in a boycott, protest or other acts of subtle or overt noncooperation and then return to their everyday lives, whereas violent insurgents often have to make enormous, and sometimes irreversible, changes to their lives based on their chosen form of struggle.

These points can be communicated through public information campaigns and institutions such as schools, universities, neighborhood associations, labor unions, religious bodies and youth clubs. They can be customized to draw on appropriate terminology, history and values of a particular society and expressed through diverse means such as literature, videos, films, television shows, advertisements, music, public performances, visual art, cultural practices, popular events and statements by respected leaders. Public education can further be supported through underwriting research about best practices and case studies of civil resistance, developing and sharing general educational resources, and translating these resources into languages spoken around the world.

A wide range of external actors can potentially play a role in such efforts. Public education activities avoid the political problem of supporting a particular movement or policy goal, and instead have the general purpose of making knowledge available, attractive and accessible to all.

2. Capacity Building for Civil Resistance Campaigns

A second form of support involves capacity building with the direct aim of helping campaigns unify, strategize and apply knowledge of civil resistance in their local context to achieve particular goals. For example, supporting strategic planning workshops and the development of movement-specific educational resources can provide opportunities for activists to deepen their skills and knowledge, and coordinate and plan together.[31]

External actors can also offer safe and neutral meeting space (within or outside of the country), support convenings of diverse leaders and dissidents from a given country, and help to expand peer-to-peer networks among new and veteran activists.[32] These efforts can strengthen social fabric, establish mentorship relationships, foster coalition growth, and build networks of trust that are critical for sustaining unity during collective action (especially after years of government-backed attempts to divide and rule).

In some cases, external actors who are close to the grassroots may also provide small amounts of funding to support movement infrastructure. This may include supporting local organizations and capacities that enable the movement to build its resource base, recruit and train new participants, develop new strategies, and coordinate efforts among different locales.

The emphasis in any such assistance should be on responding to local demand and needs by providing information, analysis and requested resources for civil resisters to use. At the same time, external actors should recognize that they lack full understanding of the local context, and thus should never become involved in specifically advising or weighing the scale in favor of particular tactics.[33] External actors may provide knowledge, networks and opportunities, but it is for local activists to decide how to use them. The only exception to this is that external actors should not hesitate to make it clear that, based on extensive amounts of evidence, engaging in violent tactics is a recipe for disaster.[34]

In addition, external actors must be cautious if they want to offer any funding, since this can lead to infighting and rivalries within a movement, siphon talent away from the grassroots, distort local engagement and agendas, and be cited by adversaries in public statements to delegitimize the movement and justify repression.[35] However, there are ways that these risks can be reduced, for example by offering in-kind contributions, issuing funding in small installments, creating more activist-friendly grant practices, allowing intermediaries with deep knowledge of the local context to guide funding, and avoiding foreign state involvement.[36]

3. Mitigating the Impact of Repression and Disruption

Disruption of business as usual and repression against a nonviolent uprising are inevitable when a movement challenges a government.

Disruption can take the form of lost wages (such as during a strike) or scarcity of goods, for example. In these cases, outsiders can provide remediation services, including strike funds for dissidents losing their capacity to support their families (unions in Europe and the United States provided such funds for Polish workers in the 1980s). They can also provide medical services via facilities inside the country or via sanctuaries outside the country.

Repression can vary in severity (from administrative penalties to violence) and scale (from a few dissidents to entire crowds during public actions). To mitigate its impacts, media and NGOs can raise the visibility of persecuted activists, legal support can be provided, and diplomats and other high-profile personnel can show solidarity by attending trials of dissidents.[37] All of these efforts can induce or compel a government to have a more transparent and fair judicial process, while possibly lightening any sentences.

In addition, when activists are under threat, urgent action and emergency response funds can provide them with the means to leave the country with their families, attend to their physical or mental health, and consider options in a safe space outside the country. In extreme cases, full relocation and support with asylum requests may be offered.

4. Raising the Cost of Repression

Repression is always costly for governments to implement, but rulers may calculate that the pros outweigh the cons. Fortunately, there are many ways for international actors to increase the cost of repression so that rulers and their agents think twice before deploying it, and are forced to endure greater losses if they choose to do so.

For example, the international human rights community does critically important work documenting abuses, "naming and shaming" perpetrators, and pursuing legal accountability. In the future when a government uses violent repression against civil resisters seeking their rights, what if automatic international investigations are started with the intent of swiftly imposing targeted sanctions (including denial of visas and freezing of assets) on specific perpetrators?[38] Such investigations could also lay the groundwork for future prosecutions.

In addition, NGOs, media outlets and governments can raise the profile of civil resistance campaigns and leaders so that a regime suffers greater public and international backlash if they are persecuted. Sympathetic governments can further make public statements warning against repression and condemning it when it happens. Countries that have

> *Diplomats can play key roles in raising the cost of repression, for example by showing up at public campaign actions as witnesses.*

significant formal and informal points of contact with foreign security services can also try to establish backchannel communications between their own officers and counterparts abroad, advising these counterparts of the costs and risks of obeying an autocrat's orders to crack down on a popular nonviolent challenge.[39]

Diplomats can play key roles as well, for example, by showing up at public campaign actions as witnesses and engaging in coordinated actions with representatives of other states.[40] Nongovernmental actors on the ground can also have a powerful deterrent effect. For example, unarmed civilian protection—in which civilians (foreign and/or local) train and deploy to sensitive areas, proactively communicate with parties in conflict, are visible witnesses, and at times negotiate and de-escalate tensions—can avert repression.[41]

Going further, governments that are sympathetic to civil resisters can threaten or implement a variety of sanctions. They can stop arms shipments and any joint military exercises or collaboration. They can lobby their allies to do the same. Under certain conditions, they may consider derecognizing regimes that are enacting widespread repression, and consider recognizing the nonviolent opposition as a more legitimate representative of a country's population.[42]

All of the above actions are more impactful when a civil resistance campaign is simultaneously waging conflict on the ground. To the extent that these external actions reduce a regime's capacity or willingness to use repression, they provide greater space for the nonviolent campaign to do its work. In addition, such actions can shift incentives for regime insiders and their allies. When supporting a regime becomes less profitable, and when the regime itself appears unsustainable, new assessments of self-interest can cause previously loyal supporters to defect.

5. Fostering a Stable Political Transition
This category of support does not apply to all civil resistance campaigns, as many seek rights- and reform-based changes, rather than full political transitions. However, for campaigns that do seek political transitions, external actors can take actions to foster and stabilize that process.

For example, external actors can meet with representatives of opposition groups, encourage them to unify around a common vision and plan, and help to facilitate this process through dialogue and negotiations. Such efforts are potentially quite important because a unified opposition is more powerful, will have a greater claim to popular legitimacy, and is more likely to lead to democratic consolidation after a transition. External actors can further incentivize this process by pledging future economic and other assistance (i.e. institution building) on the condition that a transition takes place.

External actors can also play an important role in opening up backchannels between civil resistance leaders and regime insiders to negotiate the terms of transition. Foreign states may use their points of contact with domestic regime security services to reassure them that political transition is a worthy outcome, and that there are many benefits to service under democratic governments.[43] They can also lower the costs of defecting for regime elites, for example by offering protection to whistleblowers who speak up and leave the regime.

Lastly, external actors can help to economically and politically stabilize a nation in the post-transition phase, by making good on pledges of economic assistance and technical support, and possibly deploying human rights monitors to ensure that violent retribution does not take place against previous elites.

It is also important for external actors to recognize that civil resistance in the post-transition phase may at times be necessary to hold new elites accountable, address long-standing systemic problems of corruption, and ensure that new political arrangements reflect the aspirations of the movement that drove the transition.[44] Accordingly, external actors should be ready to play a watchdog role with the new government when it confronts its own mobilized nonviolent citizenry in the future.

Applying this Framework: Re-examining Resistance and Possibilities in Syria

Considering this framework of five categories of external support, here is an example of how, if such support was coordinated and sustained, it may have impacted a real case.

In March 2011, Syrians began mass demonstrations, believing that protests similar to those in Egypt's Tahrir Square would unseat President Assad. Mobilized citizens showed amazing ingenuity, resolve and bravery, but they had had little preparation. Through civil resistance Syrians made great gains against the Assad regime in the ensuing months, shaking the government more than at any other time in the past four decades and inducing numerous defections. The growing campaign made progress despite repression, but when Assad had not left power after several months, some lost confidence in the efficacy of nonviolent tactics. The Free Syrian Army formed with an initial stated goal of protecting the nonviolent resisters, but defense soon turned into offense and the switch to violent insurgency (with some belief that the international community would support it, and possibly invoke RtoP as they had in Libya) had disastrous consequences that continue to unfold today.[45]

Consider what could have happened if outside parties had supported public educational efforts about the efficacy of nonviolent civil resistance for years prior to the 2011 uprising. The regime would have objected, but there is little basis in international law to support this objection (a topic we will discuss further), and such efforts would have been impossible to stamp out.

In the years prior to 2011, what if external actors (including Syrians living abroad) had also supported more targeted knowledge sharing about civil resistance with dissidents on the ground who had reached out and expressed interest? Perhaps a process of unification and transition planning among the opposition could have been supported on an ongoing basis as well.

What would have happened if people had prepared for a multi-year nonviolent struggle and not expected Assad to be gone within months? Research finds that the average nonviolent campaign against a regime lasts for three years, which is still far shorter than the nine-year average duration of armed insurgency.[46]

At the time of the first public protest in March 2011, what if the nonviolent campaign had received immediate and coordinated international support, and violent insurgency had not been incentivized as the primary way to secure international involvement?[47]

In the face of Assad's repression against public nonviolent actions, what if counterviolence had flared up briefly but was overwhelmingly rejected by the population and condemned by the international community? Instead, Syrians might have switched *en masse* to and sustained lower-risk tactics such as long-term targeted boycotts and work slowdowns in businesses that had connections with the regime, so that those who profited under Assad's rule continued to lose money.

> *As we consider concerns about implementing RtoA... we should also consider the costs and risks of maintaining the status quo.*

What if dissidents had been successful at unifying and articulating a transition process, which could have then been credibly communicated to regime agents who were considering defection? What if the opposition had been able to develop a widely recognized representative leadership body, and what if members of the international community had started to derecognize the Assad government and increasingly recognize this opposition body as the legitimate representative of the Syrian people?[48] What if the international community pledged economic and other forms of assistance for a post-transition Syrian government?

While some of these actions were carried out in isolation or at a small scale, we will never know how a more proactive, coordinated, sustained and appropriately-sized effort among a variety of external actors would have impacted the outcome. Such an effort would have entailed costs, risks, and technical challenges, but in hindsight it represents a far more promising path than the road that was taken. Thus, as we consider concerns about implementing RtoA in the following section, we should also consider the costs and risks of maintaining the status quo, in which authoritarian governments, often backed by powerful foreign allies, foment humanitarian catastrophes and meet popular nonviolent challenges with repression and relative impunity.

Addressing Concerns about a Right to Assist

When lives hang in the balance, any model for intervention must be subject to scrutiny. This section identifies some potential concerns with RtoA, and we welcome further research and commentary in any of these areas. Although it is beyond the scope of this piece to comprehensively evaluate every concern, we seek to address some of the primary ones. These include:

1. What campaigns should receive assistance?

2. Is support for civil resistance synonymous with supporting regime change?

3. What if external support has a harmful impact on a campaign?

4. What if external support contributes to societal instability?

5. What forms of external support to civil resistance campaigns are permissible under international law?

6. How should RtoA be invoked, and who should exercise oversight?

Concern 1. What campaigns should receive assistance?

We advocate for at least three baseline criteria for campaigns to receive assistance under RtoA. Different contexts will demand attention to different factors, and we expect additional research, practice, and context-based approaches to refine or expand this list in the future.

The three baseline criteria are:

a. A campaign is committed to nonviolent discipline

Nonviolent discipline entails using tactics that abstain from physical violence, threats of physical violence, or property destruction that has the potential to physically harm people. Maintenance of nonviolent discipline is a strategic necessity, even if a civil resistance campaign is subject to provocations and violence is used against it.

A challenge of this criterion is that it can be impossible for a campaign to ensure that every person who participates in a public action remains nonviolent. Campaigns often lack a direct command and control structure, so they cannot fully control who may show up and play a spoiler role. Regimes also frequently send undercover provocateurs to foment violence as a way to delegitimize campaigns and provide a pretext for regime repression.

Therefore, additional refinements to the nonviolent discipline criterion, based on context, are important. We argue that at a minimum a campaign should be officially and publicly committed to nonviolent tactics, call for nonviolent discipline from all supporters, take actions (such as training participants) to promote nonviolent discipline, denounce violent acts that may take place during public actions, and be able to maintain nonviolent discipline of clearly identified leaders at all public actions.

b. A campaign's goals are consistent with internationally recognized human rights

Civil resistance campaigns have a wide range of possible objectives that they may pursue at the local, regional, national or international level. The majority seek changes of policy and practice related to human rights (minority rights, indigenous rights, women's rights, labor rights); public safety and security (either from environmental degradation, criminal groups, agents of the state, or armed conflict); economic fairness; social and cultural norms; good governance (anti-corruption struggles and recognition of property rights); or democratic rule.

However, not every campaign has such goals. Some campaigns may seek to use civil resistance tactics to marginalize or harm populations (for example, by boycotting minority-owned businesses). Others may use civil resistance in support of political parties whose aims run counter to democracy and human rights.

To protect against this, as a baseline any campaign receiving support under RtoA should have practices that are clearly consistent with, and aims that advance, the rights outlined in the Universal Declaration of Human Rights.[49]

c. The civil resistance campaign is separate from a registered political party

Civil resistance campaigns often organize actions during electoral campaigns. However, it is not the role of the international community to pick election winners, and thus, external support under RtoA should not be given to political parties. The international community has an interest in supporting a free and fair democratic process, neutrality of election administration, and independent civil society monitoring of the vote. Therefore, total electoral disengagement is not a prerequisite for a campaign to receive support, but independence from political parties is.

Concern 2: Is support for civil resistance synonymous with supporting regime change?

A policy of regime change entails an external actor (generally a foreign state) taking deliberate actions with the goal of changing an incumbent government. Such an objective has generally been pursued through interstate warfare; training, arming and supporting violent insurgents; supporting a coup d'état; manipulating the information environment; and/or financing opposition groups and political parties in a variety of activities.

The Right to Assist is based on different premises. In campaigns of civil resistance, decisions about what objectives to pursue and what actions to take are made by campaign participants on the ground, rather than foreign supporters. Furthermore, such campaigns have a wide range of possible goals (many are reformist or rights-based in nature) beyond political transitions.[50]

That said, it is self-evident that some campaigns seek to change unaccountable national governments. Sometimes these campaigns start by trying to achieve reformist and rights-based goals, but when their efforts are thwarted by a government's systemic repression, corruption and incompetence, these campaigns start to seek a change of government altogether. In such circumstances, the choice is made by the campaign itself, not a foreign actor. The choice is also informed by the domestic government's actions—reforms and compromises may have led to its preservation, but obstinacy instead led to a transformation of popular demands.

Notwithstanding this dynamic, there are legitimate concerns that foreign supporters could try to foment civil resistance campaigns within a country, or manipulate a campaign's ends to achieve a foreign policy goal of regime change. We would never approve of using RtoA as a means for such efforts, and we also point out that such efforts would face considerable challenges. Civil resistance campaigns are composed of thousands or millions of people who make the personal decision to take action and mobilize (sometimes with significant sacrifice of their time, energy, material resources and personal safety). Popular legitimacy of goals, actions and communications is critical for this to happen—a campaign has to represent people's grievances and aspirations or else people stop supporting it. If at the behest of foreigners a campaign adopts an agenda that does not resonate domestically, public participation will rapidly decline.[51] Indeed, foreign support that attempts to manipulate a nonviolent campaign may be more likely to cause the campaign to fail altogether, rather than to achieve a foreigner's aims (unless those aims are, in fact, to produce failure).[52]

Concern 3: What if external support has a harmful impact on a campaign?

It can be challenging for well-intentioned external actors to discern what exact support to provide to a campaign, as well as where, when, how and to which particular groups to provide it. Campaigns are generally less structured than traditional NGOs, may have unclear lines of leadership and accountability, and depend on popular voluntary mobilization in order to succeed. There is always a risk that external support could damage a campaign, for example by reducing its legitimacy, increasing the risk of repression, or causing internal divisions among groups within it.

This topic merits further in-depth treatment, but in brief, here are some principles that external actors should consider:

1. Listen to the needs of mobilized communities

External actors should begin by seeking to understand the context in which they may become involved. Because civil resistance is a bottom-up phenomenon, this means that external actors must make efforts to identify and listen to multiple and diverse grassroots groups that are directly involved in mobilization. Any assistance should be tailored to expressed needs from people on the ground, rather than imposed.

2. Support local ownership and empowerment

Local actors lead nonviolent campaigns. They have the deepest knowledge of their situation, bear the most risk, and have the most invested in the outcome. Therefore, external support should be seen as an extension of local efforts, rather than a substitute for them. External actors need to be flexible and possibly give up a certain amount of control, allowing on the ground partners and recipients to use external support in the ways that they feel are most needed.

3. Do not give strategic or tactical advice, except for urging nonviolent discipline

Outsiders can share case studies, research findings and planning tools, and engage in Socratic dialogue with activists about prioritizing various tactics. However, because outsiders lack sufficient local knowledge, they should not give advice or advocate for particular courses of action. A single exception to this is that external actors should feel comfortable advising against the use of violence. Violence is empirically proven to be a disastrous choice for populations, and the supremacy of nonviolent tactics is established by a growing body of practice and research.

4. Coordinate support with other external actors when necessary

Integrating efforts with other external actors will often be necessary to maximize impact. There are many different forms of support that can be provided, a variety of providers and recipients of such support, and numerous other considerations such as timing and the local context. Campaigns have diverse needs, and different external actors may be best-suited to support a campaign's changing needs over time.

5. Do no harm, through action or inaction

In consultation with trusted local groups, consider the risks of harm due to both action and inaction. In some cases where external actors are getting mixed signals from the grassroots or insufficient input, it might be wise to abstain from assertive action and instead gather more information (for example about the degree to which certain external assistance may impact other local actors) or wait for the situation to ripen.

In other cases, if multiple trusted groups who are actively waging civil resistance ask for support, external actors should consider responding favorably, even if the local request is unexpected or on short notice. Local actors can determine what level of risk they are willing to tolerate and if they seek assistance, sometimes failure to take assertive action can result in harm.

Concern 4. What if external support contributes to societal instability?

Some may argue that civil resistance should not be supported because it can increase societal instability, and therefore the risk of civil war and mass atrocities. For example, two countries—Syria and Yemen—experienced nonviolent campaigns in 2011 and subsequently succumbed to violent conflict. In Syria, the nonviolent opposition was overcome by a violent flank that rapidly developed into an insurgency, while in Yemen civil resistance led to an environment where opposition groups began to press their claims with violence. These cases point to a disturbing fact: for all the promise that civil resistance can lead to democratic transitions, there is a subset of cases that highlights a major risk.

The research bears this out. Chenoweth and Stephan find that within 10 years after a national civil resistance campaign (either successful or failed) there is a 28 percent chance of civil war onset. In contrast, within 10 years after a violent campaign (either successful or failed) there is a 42 percent chance of civil war onset.[53] While the probability of civil war after a violent campaign is significantly higher, the 28 percent probability after a nonviolent campaign calls for further attention.

We need more research to determine why there are such divergent outcomes—with civil resistance showing a strong propensity to lead to democratic outcomes in the majority of cases, while approximately a quarter of cases experience a civil war at some point in the following decade. Nonetheless, several other points should be considered here as well:

a. The baseline probability of civil war under any non-democratic government (even one that is not challenged by a civil resistance movement) over a 10-year period is higher than zero.

b. Chenoweth and Stephan find that when a nonviolent or violent campaign coexists with other armed groups, the probability of post-conflict civil war over the next decade rises from 27 percent to 49 percent.[54] This is an argument for engaging in external support when a campaign is nonviolent to try to stem the development of armed splinter groups or competitors.[55]

c. Eventually political transitions happen in all countries—including non-democratic states—which generically heightens the risk of war and atrocities. What seems to be relative "peace" at the surface of non-democratic regimes obscures the suppression of pent up demand for change, which eventually gets triggered.

Thus, risk of instability that devolves into civil war or atrocities is inherent in the authoritarian model of governance. The question then is how incentivizing civil resistance might compare with alternative options. Inaction by external actors may seem to have the lowest risk at any given point in time, but lack of support for civil resistance may result in heightened volatility in the future. Without the benefit of public educational efforts and capacity building support, people may think violence is the only realistic option available to them, or a nascent nonviolent campaign may transition to violent insurgency.

Therefore, while external support may (or may not) accelerate the emergence of a campaign and possible instability, the efficacy gains from such external support— which mitigate the risk of violent conflict—may more than offset any downside risk. As policy experts Maria J. Stephan, Sadaf Lakhani and Nadia Naviwala write:

> Because outside actors probably will not be able to prevent people from engaging in protest or other direct action, particularly if they are suffering acute grievances, to minimize risk of violent instability they could invest in helping civil societies develop the capacity to organize nonviolently and maintain nonviolent discipline.[56]

Concern 5: What forms of external support to civil resistance campaigns are permissible under international law?

Addressing this question entails first determining if nonviolent civil resistance itself is protected under international law. For many nonviolent tactics, the answer is yes. Mass demonstrations, boycotts and numerous other nonviolent actions represent the exercise of human rights enshrined in various treaties, including:

- The International Covenant on Civil and Political Rights (ICCPR)
- African Charter on Human and Peoples' Rights
- The European Convention on Human Rights and Fundamental Freedoms (ECHR)
- The American Convention on Human Rights
- The Convention on the Elimination of All Forms of Racial Discrimination

More specifically, legal scholar Elizabeth A. Wilson examines the question of whether various forms of protest are protected by international human rights law and concludes that "[Nonviolent actors] are protected by... the right of self-determination, the right of peaceful assembly and various political participation rights."[57]

A more challenging question is whether there is a right to *assist* people exercising and pursuing their human rights through civil resistance. On this issue, numerous relevant international and regional treaties, UN General Assembly resolutions, and statements and practices of other international institutions (such as the Human Rights Council and other treaty-established entities) provide a basis for the argument that such a right exists.[58] Drawing from this body of law, practice, and precedent, Maina Kiai, the former UN Special Rapporteur on the Rights to Freedom of Peaceful Assembly and Association, notes that:

> The right to freedom of association not only includes the ability of individuals or legal entities to form and join an association but also to *seek, receive and use resources*—human, material and financial—from domestic, foreign, and international sources.[59] (emphasis added)

Wilson makes a similar point—that in order to be fully effectuated, some human rights are conjoined with secondary rights:

> The primary right to engage in nonviolent protest implicates political participation rights, the rights to opinion, information and expression, and rights of peaceful assembly and association.... Some of these primary rights... [correspond] to the secondary right to provide support to nonviolent actors. The right to receive information... [corresponds] to the right to impart information. The right to associate with those willing to provide support... [corresponds to] the right to associate with those who wish to receive support....[60]

The common counterargument to any form of international assistance is that sovereignty and the norm of nonintervention allow a head of state to curtail external support that it finds undesirable. However, this argument is not as comprehensive or compelling as it appears on its face. The norm of nonintervention was first conceived of as an embargo against armed intervention in other countries—it is less clear the extent to which it may embargo other forms of cross-border support, particularly the transfer of information.[61]

Furthermore, in international law the concept of state sovereignty itself can be construed as inherently residing in the population of a country, as opposed to its head of state. Thus a head of state can assert sovereignty only to the extent that its population has chances to regularly and freely express its preference to vest its sovereignty in a particular government. In the case of rulers who stifle democracy and accountability, they are hardly in the position to claim that they represent their countries' populations, and their assertions of sovereignty are faulty.[62]

Compounding this situation, there are rights of self-determination and political participation that cannot be erased by the edicts of self-proclaimed sovereigns. For example, Article 1 of the International Covenant on Civil and Political Rights (ICCPR) states that:

> All peoples have the right to self-determination. By virtue of that right they freely determine their political status and freely pursue their economic, social, and

cultural development.[63]

Article 25 states that:

> Every citizen shall have the right and the opportunity...:
>
> (a) To take part in the conduct of public affairs, directly or through freely chosen representatives;
>
> (b) To vote and to be elected at genuine periodic elections which shall be by universal and equal suffrage and shall be held by secret ballot, guaranteeing the free expression of the will of the electors;
>
> (c) To have access, on general terms of equality, to public service in his country.[64]

These are recognized human rights, and if they are to have meaning in the real world, they can be cited to argue against arbitrary claims of authoritarian sovereignty. As former Special Rapporteur Maina Kiai noted in his second thematic report to the UN Human Rights Council:

> *The protection of State sovereignty is not listed as a legitimate interest in the [ICCPR]....* States cannot refer to additional grounds, even those provided by domestic legislation, and cannot loosely interpret international obligations to restrict the right to freedom of association.... Affirming that national security is threatened when an association receives funding from [a] foreign source is not only spurious and distorted, but also in contradiction with international human rights law.... (emphasis added)

> Associations, whether domestic- or foreign-funded, should therefore be free to promote their views—even minority and dissenting views, [and] challenge governments about their human rights record or campaign for democratic reforms, without being accused of treason and other defamatory terms.[65]

Kiai further notes that "Human Rights Council resolution 22/6 calls upon States to ensure 'that no law should criminalize or delegitimize activities in defence of human rights on account of the origin of funding thereto.'"[66]

Therefore, many tactics of civil resistance are protected under international human rights law, and these rights further enable various forms of external support. At a bare minimum, domestic actors have a right to receive assistance in the form of information, and external actors have a right to provide it. Other forms of external support, such as material assistance to civil society groups pursuing and exercising their human rights, also cannot be categorically embargoed by an authoritarian's arbitrary claims of sovereignty. The burden of proof does not need to lie with those seeking to justify assistance to civil resistance campaigns. Rather, the burden should be shifted onto authoritarian governments to justify why they have a legitimate claim to sovereignty, and why they feel it is legitimate for them to contravene the rights of their populations and deny assistance.

Concern 6: How should RtoA be invoked, and who should exercise oversight?

Central questions in international affairs involve the legitimacy and oversight of foreign intervention and other international actions, and RtoA needs to be considered from this perspective as well. Under what conditions are various actions warranted, what actions are permissible, who gets to decide, and to whom are various actors accountable?

The doctrine of the Responsibility to Protect addresses these questions by basing actions on either: a) consent of the host government; or b) a trigger of mass atrocities. The latter is equated with an effective abandonment of sovereign responsibility, which in turn opens the door to the most coercive forms of direct foreign intervention. To address legitimacy and accountability concerns, RtoP is invoked in the United Nations, through which oversight is exercised.

In contrast, the Right to Assist has different trigger points, a less formal invocation process and different remedies. RtoA takes as its starting point the rights of people to access information and engage in acts of nonviolent civil resistance that are protected by international human rights law. The first category of assistance—public education—requires no formal trigger as it relates nearly exclusively to information exchange that is public and intended for society as a whole, rather than any one faction. In addition, many forms of assistance in the second category—capacity building—also fall largely within internationally protected human rights activities. These forms of support may be most impactful before a widely visible campaign has emerged, and can proceed under RtoA to groups that meet relevant criteria.

If a government threatens or engages in repression that violates the rights of nonviolent actors, then the third and fourth categories of RtoA assistance—to mitigate the impact and increase the cost of repression—may be triggered.[67]

Lastly, if a government has lost its popular legitimacy, is determined to retain its rule at all costs, and a population seeks a political transition, then the fifth category of assistance—fostering a stable transition—may be triggered.

These triggers for action are lower than those used in RtoP, but the forms of action contemplated in RtoA are also far less interventionist than those allowed under RtoP.

In terms of how RtoA would be invoked, as stated earlier, at present RtoA can be understood as a normative framework under which a variety of actors—NGOs, states, multilateral institutions and others—can organize their efforts without relying on the UN or foreign governments for official authorization or implementation. However, we welcome debate, critique

> *Part of the strength of RtoA is that while it can involve states, it can be far more flexible and not bound within an exclusively state-centered framework.*

and further research and development on this topic, which could result in a more formal or structured process in the future. Regarding the establishment of such a process, we would point out that—based on the lessons of RtoP—any process that puts veto power in the hands of any single state is likely to result in gridlock. Part of the strength of RtoA is that while it can involve states, it can be far more flexible and not bound within an exclusively state-centered framework.

In terms of oversight, we recognize that RtoA could be cited as a pretext by actors who seek to intervene for nefarious purposes—to promote destabilization of states as an end unto itself and to subvert sovereignty. As one bulwark against this, we advanced three criteria for supporting movements under RtoA, and those criteria should be expanded and refined in the future. To give the criteria more force, those who justify external support under RtoA while disregarding these criteria should be sanctioned. We also noted that when a campaign starts to follow a foreign agenda, its popular legitimacy—and thus its popular participation—may decrease. Therefore, nonviolent campaigns can wither if they succumb to foreign control, and this may limit some foreign efforts to "weaponize" them.[68]

One development that could give greater structure to RtoA would be for international law to offer status and recognition to nonviolent campaigns in the same way that it historically has for violent insurgencies. This could provide greater opportunities to apply qualifying criteria to campaigns and to exercise formal oversight of some forms of support.

International legal status and recognition for armed insurgencies is premised on the idea that sovereignty comes from a government exercising "effective control" over its population and territory. Effective control is seen as evidence that a population has acquiesced to a government's rule. Widespread armed insurgency is therefore seen as a refutation of effective control and withdrawal of acquiescence, which in the past has provided the basis for granting legal status to insurgencies that meet certain criteria.[69]

However, there is no such analogue of international legal recognition for widespread civil resistance campaigns despite the fact that, as legal scholar Elizabeth A. Wilson observes:

> The greater inclusiveness of nonviolent movements gives them greater claim to represent "the will of the people" as opposed to violent resistance groups....[70]

> When a resistance movement has evolved and become a large-scale mass movement with an inclusive platform, it can be concluded that the population has effectively (and demonstrably) withdrawn its consent from the government being recognized as legitimate by the international community.[71]

And:

> Since many of those engaged in nonviolent struggle think of it not as a negation of warfare (pacifism) but as an alternative means of waging war, it is arguable that it is more accurate to think of large-scale nonviolent civil resistance as creating a state of affairs analogous to civil war.[72]

Legal recognition of civil resistance campaigns could thus be a useful adjunct to RtoA.[73] Critically, such recognition could also incentivize the choice of nonviolent strategies of change, thereby reducing the privilege that violent uprising currently enjoys in international law, and creating a basis for greater protection of civil resistance campaigns that exercise and pursue recognition of fundamental human rights.

Conclusion

Conflict is inevitable between and among populations and governments. How these conflicts are waged determines their constructive or destructive capacity.

In the democratic ideal, tensions are channeled through a political process in which rules are clear, widely regarded as legitimate, and upheld in an impartial manner so that disputes can be addressed in constructive ways.

Under non-democratic governments, rules are often unclear, slanted, and regarded as unfair and illegitimate. This situation leads to mounting grievances and demand for a means to wage conflict outside of corrupted institutions. The choice that people make about how to fight—through nonviolent or violent tactics—has a major bearing on the risk of mass atrocities.

The Responsibility to Protect does not consider the importance of this choice, nor the power of civil resistance campaigns. RtoP is further limited by the constraints of approval of the UN Security Council, and its conception of available options to remedy atrocity risk.

In contrast, the Right to Assist recognizes that we should privilege the choice of civil resistance over armed insurrection because it reduces atrocity risk and increases the chance of stable and rights-respecting outcomes. Furthermore, RtoA does not need to be invoked by a formal vote of the UN Security Council. Rather, it is an umbrella under which a variety of actors can organize and legitimize their efforts, although RtoA may evolve into something more structured over time with future practice and debate.

The forms of support contemplated under RtoA are far less interventionist than those contemplated by Pillar 3 of the Responsibility to Protect. They primarily consist of advocacy of nonviolent strategies of change, educational and knowledge-sharing efforts, promotion of dialogue among opposition groups, some targeted forms of material support, efforts to prevent and reduce the impact of repression, and the exertion of nonviolent pressure on a movement's adversary. Such actions have grounding in past practice and international law and norms.

Any external intervention carries with it the possibility of producing detrimental outcomes. This issue must be taken seriously, and certain forms of support (such as direct state funding of civil resistance campaigns) can have a negative impact. However, such risks should not deter exploration of the positive role that external actors can play, and further research can help to develop and refine models of constructive assistance to civil resistance campaigns.

In addition, just as intervention may carry risks, so too does inaction. An outwardly stable authoritarian society may seem less likely to commit mass atrocities at a given point in time, but the risk factor rises as soon as the population starts to contend. Failing to present civil resistance as a realistic option, and failing to support populations when they choose to engage in nonviolent tactics, may increase the likelihood that they later choose violence.

Thus, when people are organizing and exercising their internationally recognized human rights to demand accountability, rights, and justice, supporting them may be the best choice of all from the perspective of reducing the likelihood of mass atrocities.

Endnotes

[1] UN General Assembly. (2005, September 16). *2005 World Summit Outcome, A/RES/60/1*, paras. 138-139.
http://www.un.org/ga/search/view_doc.asp?symbol=A/RES/60/1

[2] Summarized based on: UN General Assembly. (2009, January 12). *Implementing the Responsibility to Protect: Report of the Secretary General, A/63/677.*
https://documents-dds-ny.un.org/doc/UNDOC/GEN/N09/206/10/PDF/N0920610.
pdf?OpenElement

[3] UN Security Council. (2011, March 17). *Resolution 1973, S/RES/1973.*
http://www.un.org/en/ga/search/view_doc.asp?symbol=S/RES/1973%282011%29

[4] On April 14, 2011, US President Obama, British Prime Minister Cameron, and French President Sarkozy published a joint letter in which they stated: "It is unthinkable that someone who has tried to massacre his own people can play a part in their future government. The brave citizens of those towns that have held out against forces that have been mercilessly targeting them would face a fearful vengeance if the world accepted such an arrangement. It would be an unconscionable betrayal...."

"Furthermore, it would condemn Libya to being not only a pariah state, but a failed state too. Qaddafi has promised to carry out terrorist attacks against civilian ships and airliners. And because he has lost the consent of his people any deal that leaves him in power would lead to further chaos and lawlessness. We know from bitter experience what that would mean. Neither Europe, the region, or the world can afford a new safe haven for extremists...."

"... so long as Qaddafi is in power, NATO must maintain its operations so that civilians remain protected and the pressure on the regime builds. Then a genuine transition from dictatorship to an inclusive constitutional process can really begin, led by a new generation of leaders. In order for that transition to succeed, Qaddafi must go and go for good."

Obama, Barack, David Cameron, and Nicolas Sarkozy. (2011, April 14). Libya's Pathway to Peace. *The International Herald Tribune.*
https://www.nytimes.com/2011/04/15/opinion/15iht-edlibya15.html

[5] Libya has become unstable due to warring factions. Just six months after Qaddafi's ouster, Human Rights Watch commented that abuses (i.e. fighting, reprisals, and expulsion of residents) "appear to be so widespread and systematic that they may amount

to crimes against humanity" (Human Rights Watch, 2012).

In 2015, Alan Kuperman described the unfolding situation as follows: "In October 2013, the UN Office of the High Commissioner for Human Rights reported that the 'vast majority of the estimated 8,000 conflict-related detainees are also being held without due process.' More disturbing, Amnesty International issued a report last year that revealed their savage mistreatment: 'Detainees were subjected to prolonged beatings with plastic tubes, sticks, metal bars or cables. In some cases, they were subjected to electric shocks, suspended in contorted positions for hours, kept continuously blindfolded and shackled with their hands tied behind their backs or deprived of food and water.' The report also noted some 93 attacks on Libyan journalists in just the first nine months of 2014, 'including abductions, arbitrary arrests, assassinations, assassination attempts and assaults.' Ongoing attacks in western Libya, the report concluded, 'amount to war crimes.' As a consequence of such pervasive violence, the UN estimates that roughly 400,000 Libyans have fled their homes, a quarter of whom have left the country altogether."

Human Rights Watch. (2012, April 18). Libya: Wake-Up Call to Misrata's Leaders Torture, Killings May Amount to Crimes against Humanity.
https://www.hrw.org/news/2012/04/08/libya-wake-call-misratas-leaders

Kuperman, Alan J. (2015, March/April). Obama's Libya Debacle: How a Well-meaning Intervention Ended in Failure. *Foreign Affairs, 94*(2).
https://www.foreignaffairs.com/articles/libya/obamas-libya-debacle

[6] For example: "An interviewed FSA [Free Syrian Army] member noted that 'we did not think for a second that we are going to end up fighting for real and long. We thought we would put on a show, so the international community will come and save us the way it was in Libya. They will bomb Bashar Al Assad's Palace and bring the government down.' He added, 'when this did not happen, we found ourselves stuck in an armed struggle that we were not prepared for.'"

Bartkowski, Maciej J., and Julia Taleb. (2015). Myopia of the Syrian Struggle and Key Lessons. In Matthew Burrows and Maria J. Stephan (Eds.), Is *Authoritarianism Staging a Comeback?* (p. 137). Washington, DC: The Atlantic Council.

[7] Specia, Megan, and David E. Sanger. (2018, May 16). How the 'Libya Model' Became a Sticking Point in North Korea Nuclear Talks. *The New York Times*.
https://www.nytimes.com/2018/05/16/world/asia/north-korea-libya-model.html

[8] Scholar Alan Kuperman writes: "As Russian President Vladimir Putin complained, NATO forces 'frankly violated the UN Security Council resolution on Libya, when in-

stead of imposing the so-called no-fly zone over it they started bombing it too.' His foreign minister, Sergey Lavrov, explained that as a result, in Syria, Russia 'would never allow the Security Council to authorize anything similar to what happened in Libya.'"

Kuperman, Alan J. (2015, March/April). Obama's Libya Debacle: How a Well-meaning Intervention Ended in Failure. *Foreign Affairs, 94*(2). https://www.foreignaffairs.com/articles/libya/obamas-libya-debacle

See also:

Gutterman, Steve. (2011, June 16). UPDATE 1-Russia, China urge adherence to Libya resolutions. *Reuters*. https://www.reuters.com/article/libya-russia-china-idAFLDE75F13V20110616

[9] Bellamy, Alex J. (2011, February). Mass Atrocities and Armed Conflict: Links, Distinctions, and Implications for the Responsibility to Protect. (Policy Analysis Brief). Stanley Foundation, p. 2. https://www.stanleyfoundation.org/publications/pab/BellamyPAB22011.pdf

[10] As former UN Secretary-General Ban Ki-moon stated: "... if we do not deal with the root causes of [violent] conflict—and offer sustainable solutions—we will be left with humanitarian emergencies and peacekeeping operations without end."

Ki-Moon, Ban. (2008, January 14). *Report of the Secretary-General on the Implementation of Security Council Resolution 1625 (2005) on Conflict Prevention, Particularly in Africa, S/2008/18*. New York: United Nations Secretariat. https://undocs.org/S/2008/18

[11] Numerous studies on the relationship between civil war onset and regime type "find empirical confirmation of an 'inverted-U' relationship between level of democracy and the probability of *onset* of *internal armed conflict*" (Hegre, 2014). In other words, these studies find that hybrid regimes (which have a mix of authoritarian and democratic characteristics) correlate with the highest risk of civil war.

Such findings support the view that full democracies are significantly less likely to have civil wars than non-democracies overall. However, such findings can also be used to argue that full authoritarian rule (notwithstanding its disturbing relationship to increased risk of interstate war and human rights abuse, for example) does not significantly increase the risk of civil war.

To investigate this question further, some researchers disaggregate the broad category of "regime type" by focusing on narrower variables such as government capacity and the presence and quality of elections. These studies show the particular value that democracy and elections have on reducing the risk of civil war, as compared to fully authoritarian rule.

Looking at government capacity, and particularly indicators of government weakness, Gleditsch and Ruggeri review data from 1946-2004 and find that "greater state weakness" increases the probability of civil war onset, and when they control for this variable, they "find that democracy has a clear negative effect on the risk of civil conflict onset..." (Gleditsch and Ruggeri, 2010).

Focusing on the presence of elections and the degree of free electoral competition as a key aspect of democratic or authoritarian regimes, Bartusevičius and Skaaning analyze data from 1817-2006 and find that governments "characterized by unconstrained electoral contestation, outperform all other regime types on civil peace." Furthermore, in a challenge to the view that hybrid regimes are at higher risk for civil war than full authoritarian regimes, they find that "hybrid regimes characterized by at least nominal electoral competition are more peaceful than autocracies without elections."

Looking deeper into the question of how different types of autocratic regimes (multi-party, single-party, and non-electoral) increase civil war risk, Bartusevičius and Skaaning find that fully non-electoral regimes create the highest risk, but that autocracies that hold non-competitive elections also have a comparatively high risk, stating that: "Irrespective of their form (single- or multi-party), electoral autocracies... appear to be intrinsically conflict-prone...."

These findings lead them to conclude with an endorsement of Hegre et al.'s view that "There is a democratic civil peace" and "[t]he most reliable path to stable domestic peace in the long run is to democratize as much as possible" (Hegre et al., 2001).

Bartusevičius, Henrikas, and Svend Erik Skanning. (2018). Revisiting democratic civil peace: Electoral regimes and civil conflict. *Journal of Peace Research, 55*(5), pp. 626, 638.
https://doi.org/10.1177/0022343318765607

Gleditsch, Kristian Skrede, and Andrea Ruggeri. (2010). Political opportunity structures, democracy, and civil war. *Journal of Peace Research, 47*(3), p. 300.
https://doi.org/10.1177/0022343310362293

Hegre, Håvard. (2014). Democracy and armed conflict. *Journal of Peace Research, 51*(2), p. 160.
https://doi.org/10.1177/0022343313512852

Hegre, Håvard, Tanja Ellingsen, Scott Gates, and Nils Petter Gledissch. (2001, March). Toward a Democratic Civil Peace? Democracy, Political Change, and Civil War, 1816-1992. *American Political Science Review, 95*(1), p. 44.

[12] Scholar Erica Chenoweth finds that the onset of nonviolent campaigns striving to achieve maximalist goals (a change of government, self-determination, or expulsion of foreign occupiers) nearly doubled from the 1990s to the 2000s, and is on pace to nearly double again by the end of the current decade (2010-2019).

Onset of nonviolent campaigns seeking maximalist goals: 1900-2015

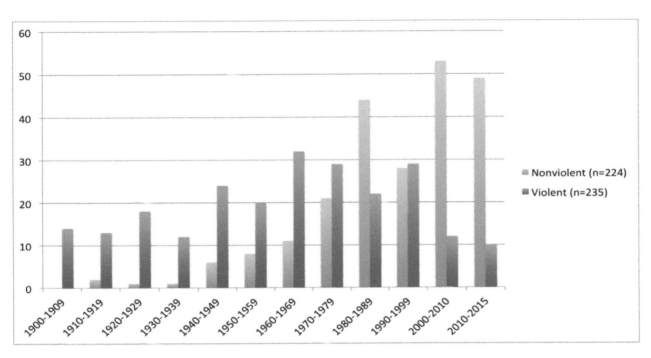

Chenoweth, Erica, and Maria J. Stephan. (2016, January 18). How the world is proving Martin Luther King right about nonviolence. *Washington Post*. https://www.washingtonpost.com/news/monkey-cage/wp/2016/01/18/how-the-world-is-proving-mlk-right-about-nonviolence/

[13] This finding is especially remarkable because nonviolent campaigns represent a greater threat to staying power of the regime than violent campaigns (as in, nonviolent campaigns have a higher success rate of leading to political transitions), so one could assume that these campaigns would be more likely to be subjected to mass killings.

Perkoski, Evan, and Erica Chenoweth. (2018). *Nonviolent Resistance and Prevention of Mass Killings During Popular Uprisings*. Washington, DC: ICNC Press, p. 8. https://www.nonviolent-conflict.org/wp-content/uploads/2017/07/nonviolent-resistance-and-prevention-of-mass-killings-perkoski-chenoweth-2018-icnc.pdf

[14] The structural risk factors listed here are found in: Harff, Barbara. (2019). Countries at risk of genocide and politicide after 2016—and why. In Barbara Harff and Ted Robert Gurr (Eds.), *Preventing Mass Atrocities: Policies and Practices* (pp. 30-31). New York and Oxon: Routledge.

[15] For a synopsis of relevant research findings, see:

Bartkowski, Maciej. (2017, September 17). Do Civil Resistance Movements Advance Democratization?. *Minds of the Movement* (blog), International Center on Nonviolent Conflict.
https://www.nonviolent-conflict.org/blog_post/civil-resistance-movements-advance-democratization/

For more information on civil resistance and democratic transitions, also see endnote 21.

[16] Scholar Stephen McLoughlin writes: "Two risk factors related to regime type and behavior significantly raise risk of mass atrocities. The first is **absence of or limitation on democracy**; the second is **limited rule of law**...." (emphasis added)

"Human rights, political stability and economic prosperity are all premised on the rule of law. When a weakening or abusive regime disregards the rule of law, particularly where democratic checks and balances are absent, a population is far more vulnerable to deprivation and discrimination. The lack of an impartial judiciary allows impunity for acts of discrimination and violence against vulnerable groups...."

"The rule of law thus points to both risk and resilience. When it is weak, the risk of mass atrocities is higher. When it is strong, the risk is diminished" (McLoughlin, 2014).

Scholar and genocide expert Barbara Harff's research finds that: "The more skewed the country is in terms of **placing full control in the hands of the few**, especially if the elite represents an ethnic minority, the greater the chances that future conflicts will lead to mass atrocities and genocide" (emphasis added) (Harff, 2019).

In terms of resilience factors that reduce atrocity risk, Stephen McLoughlin (2014) cites **"good governance"** as a major factor. Similarly, Jack Goldstone et al. find democracy to be a factor reducing the risk of "ethnic wars, revolutions, and genocides": "The key elements of **stable democracy** are to combine **fully open access to political office with fully institutionalized and functional political competition**.... Where these conditions obtain, even amidst seemingly inhospitable conditions for stability or democracy, the relative odds of ethnic wars, revolutions, and genocides have been dramatically lower" (emphasis added) (Goldstone et al., 2005).

Alex Bellamy includes "**Vibrant civil society and active private sectors**" as sources of resilience, and comments that "... excessive attention to the 'rescue fantasies' of outsiders has drawn attention away from the work of local civil societies, populations, and individuals to protect themselves. The focus of the international community needs to be placed squarely on those domestic capacities that help societies reduce underlying risk and navigate peacefully through difficult times..." (Bellamy, 2011).

Bellamy, Alex J. (2016, April). Reducing Risk, Strengthening Resilience: Toward the Structural Prevention of Atrocity Crimes. (Policy Analysis Brief). Stanley Foundation, p. 9. https://www.stanleyfoundation.org/publications/pab/Risk-Resilience-BellamyPAB416.pdf

Goldstone, Jack A., Ted Robert Gurr, Barbara Harff, Marc A. Levy, Monty G. Marshall, Robert H. Bates, Jay Ulfelder, and Mark Woodward. (2005, September). *A Global Forecasting Model of Political Instability*. Paper presented at the Annual Meeting of the American Political Science Association in Washington, DC. http://globalpolicy.gmu.edu/documents/PITF/PITFglobal.pdf

Harff, Barbara. (2019). Countries at risk of genocide and politicide after 2016—and why. In Barbara Harff and Ted Robert Gurr (Eds.), *Preventing Mass Atrocities: Policies and Practices* (p. 30). New York and London: Routledge.

McLoughlin, Stephen. (2014). *The Structural Prevention of Mass Atrocities: Understanding Risk and Resilience*. London and New York: Routledge, pp. 55-57.

[17] Chenoweth and Stephan created and used the NAVCO (Nonviolent and Violent Campaigns and Outcomes) Data Project in their work, which: "... contains a sample of resistance campaigns based on consensus data of scholars of both violent and nonviolent conflict. Resistance campaigns include campaigns for domestic regime change, against foreign occupations, or for secession or self-determination. Omitted from the data set are major social and economic campaigns, such as the civil rights movement and the populist movement in the United States. To gain inclusion into the NAVCO data set, the campaign must have a major and disruptive political objective, such as the ending of a current political regime, a foreign occupation, or secession. About ten campaigns (four nonviolent and six violent) did not fit into any of these categories but were nevertheless included in the data set."

Stephan, Maria J., and Erica Chenoweth. (2008). Why civil resistance works: The strategic logic of nonviolent conflict. *International Security, 33*(1), p. 15.

[18] Chenoweth, Erica, and Maria J. Stephan. (2011). *Why Civil Resistance Works: The Strategic Logic of Nonviolent Conflict*. New York: Columbia University Press, p. 73.

In addition, when overall success rates in the NAVCO 1.0 data set were broken down by campaign objective, the results show that civil resistance campaigns seeking political transitions against governments (rather than self-determination or expelling foreign occupiers) had a 59 percent success rate for nonviolent campaigns, versus 27 percent success rate for violent campaigns.

Stephan, Maria J., and Erica Chenoweth. (2008). Why civil resistance works: The strategic logic of nonviolent conflict. *International Security, 33*(1), p. 8.

[19] Chenoweth, Erica, and Maria J. Stephan. (2011). *Why Civil Resistance Works: The Strategic Logic of Nonviolent Conflict*. New York: Columbia University Press, pp. 213-215.

[20] *Ibid.* p. 216.

[21] Other studies on civil resistance, political transition, and democracy find that:

1. Transitions driven by civil resistance are more likely to lead to democracy than violent insurgency (Karatnycky and Ackerman, 2005; Celestino and Gleditsch, 2013).

2. Transitions driven by elites and top-down processes are less likely to result in democracy. Karatnycky and Ackerman examined 67 transitions from authoritarianism from 1972-2005 and found that 50 of these transitions were driven by "civic resistance", while only 14 were driven by top-down efforts. Moreover, 32 out of the 50 transitions (64 percent) driven by civic resistance led to fully democratic outcomes, versus only 2 out of 14 transitions (14 percent) that were driven by top-down efforts (Karatnycky and Ackerman, 2005).

3. Transitions driven by civil resistance lead to vastly more durable democracies (which persist for an average of 47 years) than transitions driven by violence (in which post-transition democracies lasted an average of 5 years) or transitions that lacked any civil resistance component (in which post-transition democracies lasted an average of 9 years) (Bayer, Bethke, and Lambach, 2016).

4. The quality of democracy following civil resistance-driven transitions is higher than for transitions that are not driven by civil resistance (Bethke and Pinckney, 2016).

5. Countries that experienced civil resistance-driven transitions are more likely to experience higher economic growth in post-transition years than countries that experienced elite, top-down driven transitions (Johnstad, 2010).

6. Within a decade of a civil resistance-driven transition, governments have been able to catch up to or exceed the world average for predicted life expectancy at birth (Stoddard, 2013).

For a synopsis of these and other findings, see: Bartkowski, Maciej. (2017, September 17). Do Civil Resistance Movements Advance Democratization?. *Minds of the Movement* (blog), International Center on Nonviolent Conflict. https://www.nonviolent-conflict.org/blog_post/civil-resistance-movements-advance-democratization/

Bayer, Markus, Felix S. Bethke, and Daniel Lambach. (2016). The democratic dividend of nonviolent resistance. *Journal of Peace Research, 53*(6), pp. 758-771. https://doi.org/10.1177/0022343316658090

Bethke, Felix S., and Jonathan Pinckney. (2016, July). *Nonviolent Resistance and Quality of Democracy*. (Working Paper Series 2016:03). V-Dem Institute, University of Gothenburg. https://www.v-dem.net/files/45/Users%20Working%20Paper%203.pdf

Celestino, Mauricio Rivera, and Kristian Skrede Gleditsch. (2013). Fresh carnations or all thorn, no rose? Nonviolent campaigns and transitions in autocracies. *Journal of Peace Research, 50*(3), pp. 385–400. https://doi.org/10.1177/0022343312469979

Johnstad, Petter Grahl. (2010). Nonviolent Democratization: A Sensitivity Analysis of How Transition Mode and Violence Impact the Durability of Democracy. *Peace and Change, 35*(3), pp. 464–482.

Karatnycky, Adrian, and Peter Ackerman. (2005). *How Freedom is Won: From Civic Resistance to Durable Democracy*. Washington, DC: Freedom House. https://freedomhouse.org/sites/default/files/How%20Freedom%20is%20Won.pdf

Stoddard, Judith. (2013). How do Major, Violent and Nonviolent Opposition Campaigns, Impact Predicted Life Expectancy at Birth?. *Stability: International Journal of Security and Development, 2*(2), p.Art. 37.

[22] Pinckney, Jonathan. (2018). *When Civil Resistance Succeeds: Building Democracy After Popular Nonviolent Uprisings*. Washington, DC: ICNC Press, p. 32.

https://www.nonviolent-conflict.org/wp-content/uploads/2018/10/When-Civil-Resistance-Succeeds-Pinckney-monograph.pdf

[23] Chenoweth, Erica, and Maria J. Stephan. (2011). *Why Civil Resistance Works: The Strategic Logic of Nonviolent Conflict*. New York: Columbia University Press, p. 62.

[24] *Ibid*. pp. 66–67.

[25] Pinckney, Jonathan. (2018). *When Civil Resistance Succeeds: Building Democracy After Popular Nonviolent Uprisings*. Washington, DC: ICNC Press, pp. 37, 39. https://www.nonviolent-conflict.org/wp-content/uploads/2018/10/When-Civil-Resistance-Succeeds-Pinckney-monograph.pdf

[26] For example, quantitative and qualitative research shows that regime type and regime strength do not determine the emergence and outcomes of civil resistance campaigns.

Chenoweth, Erica, and Maria J. Stephan. (2011). *Why Civil Resistance Works: The Strategic Logic of Nonviolent Conflict*. New York: Columbia University Press, pp. 66–68.

[27] In addition to examining the influence of regime type on the emergence and outcomes of civil resistance campaigns, Chenoweth and Stephan also examined the impact of regime strength and use of violent repression against nonviolent campaigns. They found that regime strength had no influence on campaign emergence or success and that the use of violent repression against a nonviolent campaign reduced the campaign's probability of success by 35 percent (Chenoweth and Stephan, 2011).

A 2008 Freedom House study examined how other environmental factors such as a country's level of economic development, a regime's concentration of power, and a society's level of fractionalization impact the emergence and outcomes of civil resistance campaigns and concluded that: "... neither the political nor environmental factors examined... had a statistically significant impact on the success or failure of civil resistance movements" (Marchant et al., 2008).

Chenoweth, Erica, and Maria J. Stephan. (2011). *Why Civil Resistance Works: The Strategic Logic of Nonviolent Conflict*. New York: Columbia University Press, p. 68.

Marchant, Eleanor, Adrian Karatnycky, Arch Puddington, and Christopher Walter. (2008, July). Enabling Environments for Civic Movements and the Dynamics of Democratic Transition. Special Report. Freedom House, p. 1. https://freedomhouse.org/report/special-reports/enabling-environments-civic-movements-and-dynamics-democratic-transition

[28] An example of major new research in process on this topic is:

"External Support for Nonviolent Campaigns: Data Collection and Analysis." Josef Korbel School of International Studies. Sié Chéou-Kang Center for International Security and Diplomacy.
https://www.du.edu/korbel/sie/research/chenow_external_support.html

[29] Sharp, Gene. (2003). *There are Realistic Alternatives*. Boston: The Albert Einstein Institution, p. 3.

Merriman, Hardy, and Jack DuVall. (2007). Dissolving Terrorism at Its Roots. In Ralph Summy and Senthil Ram (Eds.), *Nonviolence: An Alternative for Countering Global Terror(ism)*. Hauppauge, New York: Nova Science Publishers.
https://www.nonviolent-conflict.org/wp-content/uploads/2018/11/Dissolving-Terrorism-at-Its-Roots.pdf

[30] Chenoweth, Erica. (2016, November 21). People are in the streets protesting Donald Trump. But when does protest actually work?. *Washington Post*.
https://www.washingtonpost.com/news/monkey-cage/wp/2016/11/21/people-are-in-the-streets-protesting-donald-trump-but-when-does-protest-actually-work/

[31] In some cases, workshops and online courses could also fall under the category of "public education", depending on the manner, purposes, content, and participants who join them.

[32] By the term "dissidents", we refer to individuals who are directly (and often publicly) engaged in conflict against a state. In this paper we refer specifically to dissidents who use civil resistance (as opposed to other dissidents who may espouse violence). By the term "activists", we refer to individuals who are seeking to make significant political, economic, or social change through civil resistance. Although the terms "dissidents" and "activists" can sometimes be used interchangeably, the term "activists" is broader than "dissidents", because activists may pursue a variety of claims (rights, reforms, or fundamental change) against a variety of opponents and may be high- or low-visibility in their efforts.

[33] As Maria J. Stephan, Sadaf Lakhani, and Nadia Naviwala state: "Outside actors are never in the best position to give strategic or tactical advice to local civic actors, but they are in a position to support capacity building for strategic, disciplined nonviolent action."

Stephan, Maria J., Sadaf Lakhani, and Nadia Naviwala. (2015). Aid to Civil Society: A Movement Mindset. Special Report 361. United States Institute of Peace, p. 12.

https://www.usip.org/sites/default/files/SR361_Aid_to_Civil_Society_A_Movement_Mindset.pdf

[34] The differential in success rates of violent and nonviolent campaigns as well as the differential in democratic outcomes has already been referenced in this paper. However, there is also the question of the impact when nonviolent campaigns incorporate or exist alongside armed groups (which are termed "violent flanks"). Some argue that the presence of violent flanks may increase the chance of campaign success. However, Chenoweth and Schock found that the "average [nonviolent] campaign with a violent flank is 17% smaller than average [nonviolent] campaign without one," and since public participation is a primary factor in movement success rates, this is "evidence for an indirect negative effect, in that contemporaneous armed struggles are negatively associated with popular participation and are, consequently, correlated with reduced chances of success for otherwise-unarmed campaigns" (Chenoweth, 2016; Chenoweth and Schock, 2015).

Chenoweth and Schock further found that when an otherwise nonviolent campaign develops an intramovement violent flank (a violent group that splinters off from within a nonviolent campaign), it lowers campaign success rates from 60 percent to 41 percent (Chenoweth and Schock, 2015).

Lastly, Chenoweth and Stephan find that when a nonviolent or violent campaign co-exists with other armed groups, the probability of post-conflict civil war over the next decade rises from 27 percent to 49 percent (Chenoweth and Stephan, 2011).

Chenoweth, Erica. (2016, June 21). *Nonviolent Discipline & Violent Flanks*. Presentation at the 2016 ICNC Summer Institute at the Fletcher School of Law and Diplomacy. https://www.youtube.com/watch?v=o1-fPXqp-T8

Chenoweth, Erica and Kurt Schock. (2015). Do Contemporaneous Armed Challenges Affect the Outcomes of Mass Nonviolent Campaigns?. *Mobilization: An International quarterly, 2*(4), pp. 427, 435.

Chenoweth, Erica, and Maria J. Stephan. (2011). *Why Civil Resistance Works: The Strategic Logic of Nonviolent Conflict*. New York: Columbia University Press, p. 218.

[35] In particular, financial support from a foreign state to a nonviolent campaign can be dangerous. Examining the data on this issue, Perkoski and Chenoweth conclude that "... foreign state support... can increase the likelihood of mass killings, even in the case of a nonviolent movement."

Perkoski, Evan, and Erica Chenoweth. (2018). *Nonviolent Resistance and Prevention of*

Mass Killings During Popular Uprisings. Washington, DC: ICNC Press, p. 19. https://www.nonviolent-conflict.org/wp-content/uploads/2017/07/nonviolent-resistance-and-prevention-of-mass-killings-perkoski-chenoweth-2018-icnc.pdf

[36] While limited external funds to movements can be helpful in some contexts, our view is that external funding in general is not the key ingredient in movement success—in fact, when done excessively or with poor practice, it can lead to movement failure. In contrast, skills building, advocacy, and pressure on the campaign's adversary are all forms of non-monetary support that can have a more significant (and positive) impact.

For an excellent resource providing guidance on funding, external actors, and movements, see:

Stephan, Maria J., Sadaf Lakhani, and Nadia Naviwala. (2015). Aid to Civil Society: A Movement Mindset. Special Report 361. United States Institute of Peace. https://www.usip.org/sites/default/files/SR361_Aid_to_Civil_Society_A_Movement_Mindset.pdf

For an example of the model of movement funding and engagement used by the authors' NGO (the International Center on Nonviolent Conflict), see:

Merriman, Hardy. (2018, April 30). A Movement-centered Support Model: Considerations for Human Rights Funders and Organizations, Part I. *Minds of the Movement* (blog), International Center on Nonviolent Conflict. https://www.nonviolent-conflict.org/blog_post/movement-centered-support-model-considerations-funders-organizations/

Merriman, Hardy. (2018, May 21). A Movement-centered Support Model: Considerations for Human Rights Funders and Organizations, Part II. *Minds of the Movement* (blog), International Center on Nonviolent Conflict. https://www.nonviolent-conflict.org/blog_post/part-2-movement-centered-support-model-considerations-funders-organizations/

Merriman, Hardy. (2018, September 11). Supporting Civil Resistance Movements: Considerations for Human Rights Funders and Organizations. *Minds of the Movement* (blog), International Center on Nonviolent Conflict. https://www.nonviolent-conflict.org/blog_post/supporting-civil-resistance-movements/

Merriman, Hardy. (2019, January 10). Small Grants, Big Commitment: Reflections on Support for Grassroots Activists and Organizers. *Minds of the Movement* (blog), Inter-

national Center on Nonviolent Conflict.
https://www.nonviolent-conflict.org/blog_post/small-grants-big-commitment-reflections-support-grassroots-human-rights-activists-organizers/

[37] This is just one of many actions that diplomats can take to incorporate a more movement-centered approach into their work. For a broader discussion of other options and case studies of diplomats engaging with dissidents, civil society, and nonviolent campaigns, see:

Kinsman, Jeremy and Kurt Bassuener (Eds.). (2016). *A Diplomat's Handbook for Democracy Development Support.* Waterloo, ON: CIGI Press.

In addition, professional incentives and training for diplomats could be altered to prepare them for and reward such actions: "Diplomats should be empowered to reach out directly to civil society actors. To this end, the United States and other democracies ought to realign professional incentives for foreign service officers to reward those who facilitate collaboration and partnerships with civil society actors in the field, as well as extend the length of field rotations to enable such relationships to develop."

Lagon, Mark, and Patrick McCormick. (2015, January). The Responsibility to Accompany: A Framework for Multilateral Support of Grassroots Nonviolent Resistance. *Ethics and International Affairs.*
https://www.ethicsandinternationalaffairs.org/2015/the-responsibility-to-accompany-a-framework-for-multilateral-support-of-grassroots-nonviolent-resistance/

[38] As one possibility, Jane Mansbridge and Chibli Mallat propose a tiered response system based on levels of repression:

"We need a set of automatic triggers based on an international assessment of the level of violence that a dictatorial government is using against nonviolent protest. The exact form of the triggers is less important than the principle of reaction. The international community should begin thinking immediately about the appropriate outside responses when a dictatorial regime begins to shoot nonviolent protesters in cold blood. The UN, or one or more regional alliances, could set up an ongoing commission mandated to investigate deaths in nonviolent protests within its area of jurisdiction. One claim of such a death might produce attention to the problem. Ten claimed deaths, with some corroboration from outside sources, might generate a small task force mandated to investigate the issue. Fifty claimed deaths, with significant corroboration from outside sources, might trigger the formation of a formal committee of inquiry. One hundred corroborated deaths might trigger a formal investigation. And 200 corroborated deaths might trigger taking the issue to the UN Security Council (UNSC) for consideration of UN sanctions or sanctions by regional alliances if UN action is vetoed."

Mallat, Chibli, and Jane Mansbridge. (2012, September 11). Outside Intervention in Nonviolent Revolutions. *JURIST – Forum*.
http://jurist.org/forum/2012/09/mallat-mansbridge-nonviolent-intervention.php

[39] Admiral Dennis Blair outlines a constructive role for militaries serving in democracies, urging them to use their points of human contact with their foreign counterparts to emphasize the virtues of serving democratic rulers and advising restraint by those who may be ordered to repress popular nonviolent challenges.

Blair, Dennis. (2013). *Military Engagement Influencing Armed Forces Worldwide to Support Democratic Transitions, Vol. I and II*. Washington, DC: Brookings Institution.

Vol I opening chapter:
https://www.brookings.edu/wp-content/uploads/2016/07/militaryengagement_chapter.pdf

Vol II opening chapter:
https://www.brookings.edu/wp-content/uploads/2016/07/miltaryengagement2_samplechapter.pdf

[40] See endnote 37.

[41] According to the "Policy on Child Protection in United Nations Peace Operations":

"Unarmed civilian protection refers to a strategy for the protection of civilians, localized violence reduction and supporting local peace infrastructures, in which unarmed, trained civilians live and work with local civil society in areas of violent conflict. The High Level Independent Panel on Peace Operations recommended that unarmed approaches must be at the forefront of United Nations efforts to protect civilians, including children."

UN Department of Peacekeeping Operations, Department of Field Support and Department of Political Affairs. (2017, June). *Policy on Child Protection in United Nations Peace Operations, Ref. 2017.11*. New York.
https://dag.un.org/handle/11176/400655

For additional information on unarmed civilian protection, see:

Furnari, Ellen. (2016). *Wielding Nonviolence in the Midst of Violence: Case Studies of Good Practices in UCP*. Norderstedt: Books on Demand.

Nonviolent Peaceforce and the UN Institute for Training and Research. (2017). *Un-*

armed Civilian Protection: Strengthening Civilian Capacities to Protect Civilians Against Violence.
https://nonviolentpeaceforce.sharepoint.com/NP-US%20Documents/Shared%20
Documents/Forms/AllItems.aspx?id=%2FNP%2DUS%20Documents%2FShared%20
Documents%2FCOMMUNICATIONS%2FProgram%20Documents%2FUCP%20Train-
ing%2FUCP%5F17%2E2%20May%20copyEdited2%2Epdf&parent=%2FNP%2DUS%20
Documents%2FShared%20Documents%2FCOMMUNICATIONS%2FProgram%20Docu-
ments%2FUCP%20Training&p=true&slrid=42bba99e-1020-7000-7d26-dbbf6a0ca4fb

[42] Danny Auron explores derecognition from an international legal perspective, and argues for: "... the use of recognition policy—derecognition of existing regimes and the possible substitute recognition of nonviolent opposition forces—as a novel approach to non-physical intervention, prevention, and regime change. Such policy would assist in the termination of administrations that face mass opposition from their population and meet this resistance with systematized violence" (Auron, 2013).

For an example of how derecognition might work, Mallat et al. advocated for derecog-nition of the Syrian government and recognition of the opposing Syrian National Council (SNC): "First steps would include **surrendering the Syrian embassies to the opposition** as a far more legitimate representative of Syria's people than the present envoys. This measure would immediately promote defections in those embassies and in the Syrian diplomatic services. Should FS [Friends of Syria] governments decide that giving the embassy to the Syrian people as represented transitionally by the opposition is not sufficiently supported by consular law, they can simply **expel the local Syrian ambassador and top aides at the embassy**."

"They can also provide serious logistics to assist the SNC as the most significant um-brella group for this transitional period, in order to better advance the agenda of Syrian democracy...."

"The **U.N. General Assembly can meet again to vote formally for such recognition. Individual governments can start the process immediately**. Governments are free under international law to recognize the foreign government they consider legitimate in a given country...."

"... Many Syrians have been deprived of travel documents for years. This hampers their action and increases the risks on their lives. These Syrians should be **issued passports by the SNC government and their passports recognized for travel abroad by the FS**."

"... **Party leaders across the political spectrum of FS societies should meet with des-ignated representatives of the opposition and offer them headquarters, logistical, and media support**."

"Parliaments in supportive countries in the seventy-strong FS group can also play a key role by organizing open debates and working meetings where nonviolent revolutionary Syrians can be heard and their requests studied and discussed seriously, both for immediate needs and in preparation for the transition to democracy. The U.N. Secretariat and the Arab League.... should address the SNC and the resistance inside the country as the only worthy interlocutors for Syrian society until free elections are possible, that is, after Asad is removed from power" (emphasis added) (Mallat et al., 2012).

Auron, Danny. (2013). The Derecognition Approach: Government, Illegality, Recognition, and Non-Violent Regime Change. *George Washington International Law Review 45*(3), p. 443.

Mallat, Chibli, Jane Mansbridge, Sadek Jalal al-Azm, Trudi Hodges, Mansoor al-Jamri, Ishac Diwan, Sharhabeel al-Zaeem, John J. Donohue, and Yang Jianli. (2012, March). A Strategy for Syria Under International Law: How to End the Asad Dictatorship while Restoring Nonviolence to the Syrian Revolution. *Harvard International Law Journal, 53*, pp. 148-149.
http://www.harvardilj.org/wp-content/uploads/2012/03/HILJ-Online_53_Mallat_et_al.pdf

[43] See endnote 39.

[44] For research on the role of civil resistance in producing stability or instability in the post-transition phase, see:

Pinckney, Jonathan. (2018). *When Civil Resistance Succeeds: Building Democracy After Popular Nonviolent Uprisings.* Washington, DC: ICNC Press.
https://www.nonviolent-conflict.org/wp-content/uploads/2018/10/When-Civil-Resistance-Succeeds-Pinckney-monograph.pdf

[45] According to Mohja Kahf, "Death tolls in Syria after the uprising's militarization skyrocketed, from an unbearable five or six to thirty victims of regime fire per day in the nonviolent phase, to seventy to three hundred victims of regime fire per day."

Kahf, Mohja. (2013). *Then and Now: The Syrian Revolution to Date.* St. Paul: Friends for a Nonviolent World, pp. 16–17.
http://www.fnvw.org/vertical/Sites/%7B8182BD6D-7C3B-4C35-B7F8-F4FD486C7CB-D%7D/uploads/Syria_Special_Report-web.pdf

[46] Chenoweth, Erica, and Maria J. Stephan. (2014, July-August). Drop your weapons: when and why civil resistance works. *Foreign Affairs, 93*(4).

[47] As Mansbridge and Mallat observed in 2012: "The recent revolutions in Libya and Syria offer a bitter lesson: to generate outside intervention against a dictator, armed rebellion is more effective than even the most heroic nonviolence...."

Mallat, Chibli, and Jane Mansbridge. (2012, September 11). Outside Intervention in Nonviolent Revolutions. *JURIST – Forum.*
http://jurist.org/forum/2012/09/mallat-mansbridge-nonviolent-intervention.php

[48] For an example of what derecognition in Syria may have entailed, see endnote 42.

[49] To take this one step further, Wilson offers criteria to evaluate if a campaign can be characterized as a human rights movement. These criteria include four "general principles of nondiscrimination, nonrepression, nonexploitation, and nonviolence. If civil resistance movements manifest these principles, or some of them without negating the others, then arguably is it appropriate to characterize them as human rights movements."

Wilson, Elizabeth A. (2017). *People Power Movements and International Human Rights: Creating a Legal Framework.* Washington, DC: ICNC Press, pp. 53–58, 90–107.
https://www.nonviolent-conflict.org/wp-content/uploads/2017/11/People-Power-Movements-and-International-Human-Rights_Elizabeth-A-Wilson_2017.pdf

[50] Ironically, despite the prevalence of campaigns seeking rights-based and reformist goals, the field of civil resistance currently has more quantitative data about campaigns directly trying to change governments, which were cited earlier in this paper, likely because these campaigns have been easiest to count, classify, and compare (thus lending themselves to quantitative analysis). However, this should not overshadow the fact that many campaigns seek different ends than a political transition.

[51] On this subject, Bartkowski examined the impact of a few known Kremlin attempts to foment grassroots mobilization (particularly protests) in the United States, and concluded that:

"The Kremlin's efforts to manipulate protest potential in the United States have been only partly successful online and largely unsuccessful on the ground. What the Kremlin's interference in the U.S. proved is that a significant popular, mass-based discontent cannot be instigated on the streets without authentic grassroots drivers."

He notes that the times when "Russian trolls were more successful, though still fell short of making any type of revolutionary waves on the ground, was with earning thousands of 'likes' under posts on their fake Facebook pages (this engagement did not translate into comparable levels of participation on the streets)... or when their call for protests essentially bandwagoned on already happening movements."

He further states that "Attempts to manufacture protests failed miserably when specific issues promoted by Russian agents were not viewed by communities as amounting to a genuine grievance. For example, Russian-instigated dueling protests near the Islamic Da'wah Center of Houston, Texas on May 21, 2016 involving 'Stop Islamification of Texas' and a counter demonstration 'Save Islamic Knowledge' brought out, based on witness accounts, only a few participants: 10 and 50 respectively. This shows how difficult, if not impossible, it is to stage a mass protest from outside without tapping into an already existing sentiment and pre-existing readiness of a community to demonstrate for a specific galvanizing cause...."

Bartkowski, Maciej. (2018). The Case for Civil Resistance to Russia's Populace-Centric Warfare. *Free Russia Foundation*, pp. 14–15. https://www.4freerussia.org/the-case-for-civil-resistance-to-russias-populace-centric-warfare/

[52] We recognize that state sponsorship is an identified factor in the success rates of violent insurgencies, and that through material support states may exercise some control over these insurgencies. However, it should not be extrapolated that this same relationship applies as well to nonviolent campaigns. For example, Chenoweth and Stephan find that the presence of a foreign state sponsor increased the probability of violent campaigns' success by about 15 percent, but the presence of foreign state material support for nonviolent campaigns did not positively or negatively affect their outcomes (Chenoweth and Stephan, 2011).

Foreign state material support also creates real risks, as Chenoweth and Perkoski find that regarding campaigns in general (both violent and nonviolent): "... states are nearly 25 times more likely to crack down on civilians when... [a] dissident campaign receives foreign state support...."

Also see endnotes 35 and 51.

Chenoweth, Erica, and Maria J. Stephan. (2011). *Why Civil Resistance Works: The Strategic Logic of Nonviolent Conflict*. New York: Columbia University Press, p. 59.

Perkoski, Evan, and Erica Chenoweth. (2018). *Nonviolent Resistance and Prevention of Mass Killings During Popular Uprisings*. Washington, DC: ICNC Press, p. 18. https://www.nonviolent-conflict.org/wp-content/uploads/2017/07/nonviolent-resistance-and-prevention-of-mass-killings-perkoski-chenoweth-2018-icnc.pdf

[53] Chenoweth, Erica, and Maria J. Stephan. (2011). *Why Civil Resistance Works: The*

Strategic Logic of Nonviolent Conflict. New York: Columbia University Press, p. 216.

[54] *Ibid.* p. 218.

[55] This also points to the fact that models that look at undifferentiated "revolution" or "rapid political transition" as a driver of political instability and risk factor for civil war and mass atrocities are missing a key point—the methods (nonviolent or violent) used to achieve political transition may hold as much or more significance as the fact of the transition itself.

[56] Stephan, Maria J., Sadaf Lakhani, and Nadia Naviwala. (2015). Aid to Civil Society: A Movement Mindset. Special Report 361. United States Institute of Peace, p. 11. https://www.usip.org/sites/default/files/SR361_Aid_to_Civil_Society_A_Movement_Mindset.pdf

[57] Wilson, Elizabeth. (2015). International Legal Basis of Support for Nonviolent Activists and Movements. In Matthew Burrows and Maria J. Stephan (Eds.), *Is Authoritarianism Staging a Comeback?* (p. 160). Washington, DC: The Atlantic Council.

In a subsequent work, Wilson lists rights from the ICCPR that "a movement can invoke and exercise while waging their nonviolent struggle", including:

Collective rights
Article 1 (self-determination)

Expressive and associational rights
Article 18 (freedom of thought, conscience and religions);
Article 19 (freedom of opinion and expression);
Article 21 (freedom of peaceful assembly);
Article 22 (freedom of association);
Article 25 (right to political participation)

Bodily integrity rights
Article 6 (right to life);
Article 7 (freedom from torture; cruel, inhuman and degrading treatment);
Article 9 (liberty and security; freedom from arbitrary arrest and detention);
Article 10 (dignity)

Wilson, Elizabeth A. (2017). *People Power Movements and International Human Rights: Creating a Legal Framework.* Washington, DC: ICNC Press, p. 66.

[58] Such treaties include: the International Convention on Civil and Political Rights (IC-

CPR), the African Charter on Human and Peoples' Rights, the European Convention on Human Rights and Fundamental Freedoms (ECHR), the American Convention on Human Rights, and the Convention on the Elimination of All Forms of Racial Discrimination. UN General Assembly resolutions include the Universal Declaration of Human Rights, and the Declaration on the Right and Responsibility of Individuals, Groups and Organs of Society to Promote and Protect Universally Recognized Human Rights and Fundamental Freedoms (Declaration on Human Rights Defenders). International institutions include the Human Rights Committee, the United National Human Rights Council, and the International Labor Organization.

See: Wilson, Elizabeth. (2015). International Legal Basis of Support for Nonviolent Activists and Movements. In Matthew Burrows and Maria J. Stephan (Eds.), *Is Authoritarianism Staging a Comeback?*. Washington, DC: The Atlantic Council.

[59] Kiai, Maina. *Report of the Special Rapporteur on the Rights to Freedom of Peaceful Assembly and of Association, A/HRC/23/39*, para. 8.

[60] Wilson, Elizabeth. (2015). International Legal Basis of Support for Nonviolent Activists and Movements. In Matthew Burrows and Maria J. Stephan (Eds.), *Is Authoritarianism Staging a Comeback?* (pp. 159-60). Washington, DC: The Atlantic Council.

[61] Ackerman, Peter, and Michael J. Glennon. (2007, September 1). The Right Side of the Law. *The American Interest, 3*(1).
https://www.the-american-interest.com/2007/09/01/the-right-side-of-the-law/

[62] As Peter Ackerman and Michael Glennon write: "Contemporary autocrats hide behind principles of sovereignty and its corollary prohibition against meddling in a state's internal affairs—international legal norms that emerged when moveable type was cutting-edge technology. Their argument no longer works as it did in Gutenberg's day. State sovereignty remains an important pillar in the structure of international law, but the notion that sovereignty resides in the head of state gave way long ago to recognition that it rests in a nation's people. The scope of sovereignty narrowed further in the 20th century, as a large body of law came to protect internationally recognized human rights. And with the number of electoral democracies nearly doubling in the past twenty years, an emerging right to democratic governance has become the centerpiece of human rights law."

Ackerman, Peter, and Michael J. Glennon. (2007, September 1). The Right Side of the Law. *The American Interest, 3*(1).
https://www.the-american-interest.com/2007/09/01/the-right-side-of-the-law/

[63] ICCPR, Art. 1(1).

[64] ICCPR, Art. 25.

[65] Kiai, Maina. *Report of the Special Rapporteur on the Rights to Freedom of Peaceful Assembly and of Association, A/HRC/23/39*, paras. 30, 32.

[66] *Ibid.* para. 31.

[67] For an example, see endnote 38.

[68] See endnotes 35, 51, and 52.

[69] International law has given status to violent insurgents under the following criteria: "First, there must exist within the State an armed conflict of a general (as distinguished from a purely local) character; secondly, the insurgents must occupy and administer a substantial portion of national territory; thirdly, they must conduct the hostilities in accordance with the rules of war and through organized armed forces acting under a responsible authority; fourthly, there must exist circumstances which make it necessary for outside States to define their attitude by means of recognition of belligerency."

Lauterpacht, Hersch. (1947). *Recognition in International Law*, pp. 176–78. As cited in: Wilson, Elizabeth. (2015). 'People Power' and the Problem of Sovereignty in International Law. *Duke Journal of Comparative & International Law, 26*(5).

[70] Wilson, Elizabeth. (2015). 'People Power' and the Problem of Sovereignty in International Law. *Duke Journal of Comparative & International Law, 26*(5), p. 585.

[71] *Ibid.* p. 586.

[72] *Ibid.* p. 587.

[73] Two sources that explore this issue more fully are:

Wilson, Elizabeth. (2015). 'People Power' and the Problem of Sovereignty in International Law. *Duke Journal of Comparative & International Law, 26*(5).

Wilson, Elizabeth A. (2017). *People Power Movements and International Human Rights: Creating a Legal Framework.* Washington, DC: ICNC Press. https://www.nonviolent-conflict.org/wp-content/uploads/2017/11/People-Power-Movements-and-International-Human-Rights_Elizabeth-A-Wilson_2017.pdf

Acknowledgments

We are grateful for comments on earlier drafts of this report from Maciej Bartkowski, Erica Chenoweth, Larry Diamond, Amber French, Chibli Mallat, Jane Mansbridge, Jason Marczak, Chris Miller, Maria Stephan, Tabatha Thompson, Rosarie Tucci, Paula Garcia Tufro and Lawrence Woocher. We also want to thank Julia Constantine for copyediting and publication support.

CPSIA information can be obtained
at www.ICGtesting.com
Printed in the USA
BVHW020428100919
558008BV00003B/4/P

9 781943 271177